Sex

Wheels

About Starters Science books

STARTERS SCIENCE books are designed to encourage scientific awareness in young children. The series aims to focus the instinctive curiosity of children and to encourage exploration and experiment. It also aims to develop language, encourage discussion and suggest situations where children can examine similarities and differences.

   The text of each book is simple enough for children to read for themselves, and the vocabulary has been controlled to ensure that about 90 per cent of the words used will be familiar to them. Each book also contains a picture index and a page of notes for parents and teachers.

Written and planned by Albert James
Illustrator: Peter Edwards

A MACDONALD BOOK

© Macdonald & Co (Publishers) Ltd 1973

First published in
Great Britain in 1973

Reprinted 1974, 1983 and 1986

Printed and bound in Great Britain by
Hazell, Watson & Viney Ltd
Aylesbury, Buckinghamshire

Published by Macdonald & Co (Publishers) Ltd
Greater London House
Hampstead Road
London NW1 7QX

Members of BPCC plc

British Library Cataloguing in Publication Data
James, Albert
Wheels. — (Starters science)
   1. Readers — 1950 —
   I. Title II. Series
   428.6   PE1119

   ISBN 0-356-04443-2
   ISBN 0-356-09276-3 Pbk

STARTERS
SCIENCE

Wheels

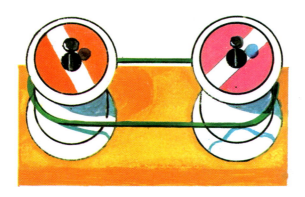

Macdonald

Everybody has come to do shopping.
The town is full of traffic.

2

All the traffic moves on wheels.
Can you find the things on wheels
in this picture?

3

This girl has to move a heavy box.
First she tries pulling it.
Then she tries rollers underneath.
She uses round sticks for rollers.
4

Then she puts the box
on a trolley with wheels.
Which way would be the easiest?
Try it and see.

Try making some carts
with wheels of different shapes.
6

This car rests on axles.
The axle is in the centre of the wheel.
What happens when an axle
is not in the centre?

7

Here is a clown on a cycle.
His cycle has one wheel.
What else has one wheel?
8

Make lists of all the things you know
with one, two, three, four
or more than four wheels.
Which list is longest?

Big
wheel

windmill

potter's
wheel

Wheels can be used for moving things
along the ground.
Wheels can be used in other ways.
10

water
wheel

pulley
wheel

spinning
wheel

Can you see what these wheels do?
Do you know what a windmill does?
Or how a water wheel works?

11

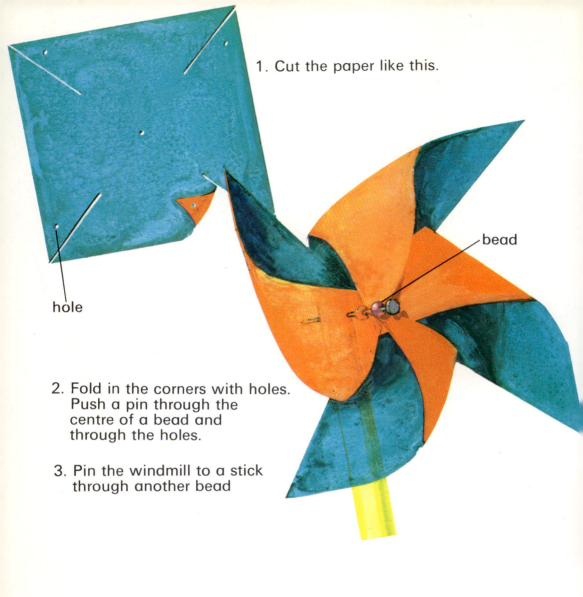

1. Cut the paper like this.

bead

hole

2. Fold in the corners with holes.
   Push a pin through the
   centre of a bead and
   through the holes.

3. Pin the windmill to a stick
   through another bead

This wheel is easy to make.

12

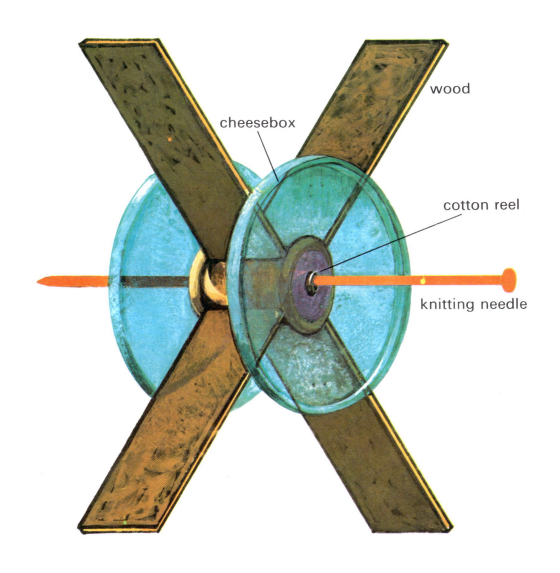

wood

cheesebox

cotton reel

knitting needle

So is this water wheel.
Remember to use a good glue.

13

Hold your water wheel under the tap.
Let the water run gently on to the vanes.
Then squirt water on to the wheel.

14

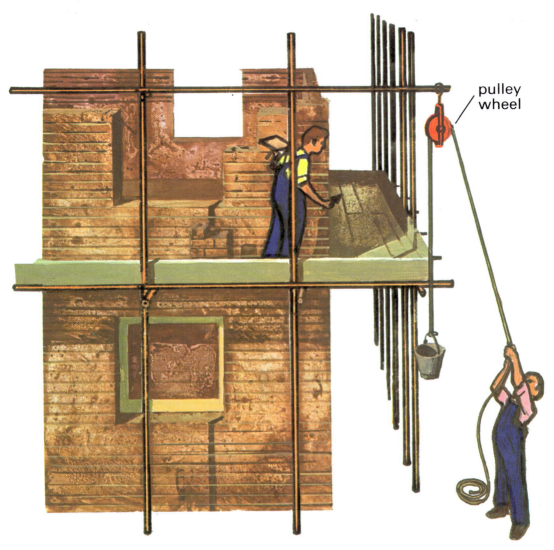

pulley wheel

This builder uses a pulley wheel.
Pulley wheels have a groove for the rope.
Can you see how the pulley helps
the builder?

15

wire

You can make a pulley
from an empty cotton reel.
Try lifting things with the pulley.
16

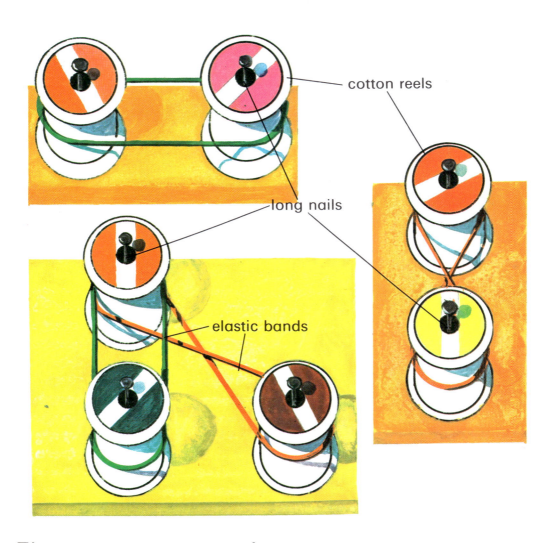

cotton reels

long nails

elastic bands

Fix some cotton reels
on to some wood, like this.
Turn one of them.
Which way do the others turn?

17

Here is the inside
of a clock.
These wheels
are called gear wheels.

18

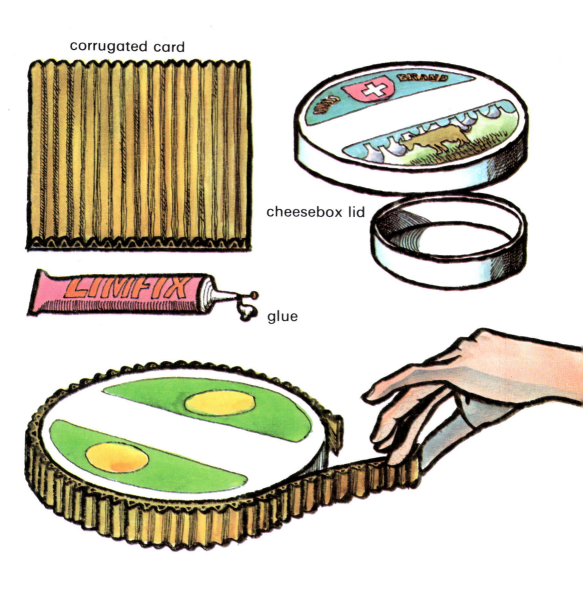

corrugated card

cheesebox lid

glue

You can make gear wheels like this.

19

If you turn one gear wheel,
which way do the others go?

20

Turn the big wheel once.
How many times does the little wheel turn?
Is the little wheel faster or slower
than the big wheel?

21

These machines have gear wheels.
Find out which way each part turns.

22

How far do you go for one turn
of your cycle wheel?
How many turns of the wheel
to go along the path?

Make some colour wheels
from card and string.
Paint them with different patches of colour.

24

Can you spin your colour wheel?
What happens to the colours
when the wheel spins?

25

People made wheels long ago.
Here are some old wheels.

26

Here are some modern wheels.
Are they the same as the old wheels?
What are they made of?

Index

traffic
(page 2)

water wheel
(page 11)

rollers
(page 4)

vanes
(page 14)

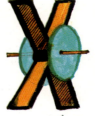

trolley
(page 5)

pulley wheel
(page 15)

axle
(page 7)

groove
(page 15)

windmill
(page 11)

gear wheel
(page 18)

Notes for Parents and Teachers

Starters Science books are designed for children to read and study on their own, but children would also benefit by sharing these topics with a parent or teacher. These brief notes explain the scientific ideas contained in the book, and help the interested adult to expand the themes.

2–5   Children can observe different uses for wheels, and their frequent appearance in everyday life; as well as how wheels make for ease of movement.

6–7   Through projects and experiments, children can discover the effect of the shape of wheels and the position of the axle on their movement.

8–14   Practical experiments and observations of different types of wheels and their functions. There are pictures of vehicles with varying numbers of wheels; wheels turning other wheels as part of machinery; and waterwheels and windmills.

15–20   Children are encouraged to learn about pulley wheels, their value and function, by observation and the construction of simple models.

21–23   The principle of gear wheels is shown by simple projects which also illustrate the comparative rate of rotation of big and small wheels. The idea of circumference as a linear measurement is clarified by the observation of wheel movement.

24–25   Making colour wheels to give experience of the merging of colours and patterns by spinning.

26–27   A comparison of the structure, material and design of old and modern wheels.